IMAGES
of Sport

CAMBRIDGE UNITED
FOOTBALL CLUB

Holders
Southern League R.A. Cup.
Culey Cup.
Cambs. F.A. Youth Cup.

Winners
1960-61 Southern League 1 Div. R.A. Cup.
1961-62 Southern League Cup.
East Anglian Cup.

Cambridge United
Football Club Ltd.
ABBEY STADIUM

Friendly
Cambridge United
v.
Hapoel Tel·Aviv
Thurs 5 Sep 1963
k.o 7.15 pm

Lucky
Programme
No

Price
4ᴰ

Cambridge United's first game against international opposition was a friendly in 1963 against Hapoel Tel-Aviv, the runners-up in the Israeli First Division. Under the newly installed floodlighting, two goals from Norman Bleanch and one from Jim Sharkey gained an impressive draw against a side that included seven current Israel internationals. The artist's impression shows that nearly forty years later nothing had changed except the shirts and the haircuts.

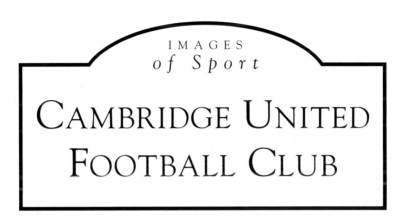

IMAGES
of Sport

CAMBRIDGE UNITED
FOOTBALL CLUB

Compiled by
Brian Attmore & Graham Nurse

TEMPUS

First published 2001
Copyright © Brian Attmore and Graham Nurse, 2001

Tempus Publishing Limited
The Mill, Brimscombe Port,
Stroud, Gloucestershire, GL5 2QG

ISBN 0 7524 2256 1

Typesetting and origination by
Tempus Publishing Limited
Printed in Great Britain by
Midway Colour Print, Wiltshire

Also available from Tempus Publishing:

0 7524 2248 0	Accrington Stanley: Images	Phil Whalley	£10.99
0 7524 1862 9	Birmingham City: Images	Tony Matthews	£9.99
0 7524 2249 9	Bristol City 1967-2001: Images	Tom Hopegood	£10.99
0 7524 2068 2	Cardiff City 1971-2000: Images	Richard Shepherd	£9.99
0 7524 1545 X	Crewe Alexandra : Images	Harold Finch	£9.99
0 7524 2176 X	Crystal Palace: Greats	Revd Nigel Sands	£12.00
0 7524 2189 1	Doncaster Rovers: Images	Peter Tuffrey	£10.99
0 7524 2259 6	Everton 1880-1945: Images	John Rowlands	£10.99
0 7524 1855 6	The Football Programme	John Litster	£12.99
0 7524 2042 9	Forever England	Mark Shaoul & Tony Williamson	£16.99
0 7524 2243 X	Gillingham: Men Who Made	Roger Triggs	£19.99
0 7524 2152 2	Ipswich Town: Images	Tony Garnett	£9.99
0 7524 2043 7	Leeds United in Europe	David Saffer	£9.99
0 7524 2094 1	Leyton Orient: Images	Neilson Kaufman	£9.99
0 7524 2255 3	Manchester City: Classics	Andrew Waldon	£12.00
0 7524 2085 2	Manchester City: Images	David Saffer & Andrew Waldon	£9.99
0 7524 1849 1	Millwall 1884-1939: Images	Millwall FC Museum	£9.99
0 7524 2187 5	Millwall 1940-2001: Images	Millwall FC Museum	£10.99
0 7524 1671 5	Northampton Town: Images	John Watson & David Walden	£9.99
0 7524 2266 9	Norwich FC: Images	Gary Enderby	£10.99
0 7524 1604 9	Queens Park Rangers: Images	Tony Williamson	£9.99
0 7524 2081 X	Reading: Greats	David Downs	£12.00
0 7524 1670 7	Rotherham United: Images	Gerry Somerton	£9.99
0 7524 2264 2	Sheffield United: Greats	Denis Clarebrough	£12.00
0 7524 2177 8	Southend United: Greats	Peter Miles & Dave Goody	£12.00
0 7524 1133 0	Swansea Town 1912-1964: Images	Richard Shepherd	£9.99
0 7524 2093 3	Swindon Town: Images	Richard Mattick	£9.99
0 7524 2044 5	Tottenham Hotspur 1882-1952: Images	Roy Brazier	£9.99
0 7524 1592 1	Vetch Field Voices	Keith Haynes	£9.99
0 7524 2091 7	Walsall: Images	Geoff Allman	£9.99
0 7524 2226 X	Wallsall: Greats	Geoff Allman	£12.00
0 7524 2056 9	West Brom Albion: Images	Tony Matthews	£9.99
0 7524 2265 0	Wolverhampton Wanderers: Greats	Tony Matthews	£12.00
0 7524 2045 3	1966 World Cup	Norman Shiel	£9.99
0 7524 1899 8	Wrexham: Images	Gareth Davies & Peter Jones	£9.99
0 7524 1568 9	York City: Images	David Batters	£9.99

Contents

Brian Attmore first appeared at the Abbey when his father took him and his brother, Stephen, in 1960. They became regulars at first and reserve team games, which helps account for his encyclopaedic knowledge of United and their players. In June 1970 he was one of the fans who were at Royston to welcome the League's newest club back from a tour of Germany, and escorted his boyhood heroes to the Guildhall for the civic reception. For many years, Brian has been actively involved with fans' organisations both at Cambridge United and nationally. He is chairman of Cambridge United Supporters Association and a founder-member of the supporters' trust, Cambridge Fans United. As a leader of the fans' protest in 2000, he handed out thousands of yellow cards waved by the crowd at a match to highlight their impatience with the Council's 'time wasting' over the stadium redevelopment plans. If any fan wants to say anything to anybody in any position of authority anywhere at Cambridge United, they are always pointed in his direction. A keen cyclist, he campaigned for cycle racks at the Abbey Stadium. Brian is a manager at the large supermarket between the Allotments End and his home in Queen Edith's. As an exceptionally good father, he takes his daughter Michelle and son Mark to every home game.

Graham Nurse moved to Cambridge in 1966 and, after watching three games at Cambridge City, took up residence at the Abbey. After two seasons at the Newmarket Road End, he got married, bought a house five minutes walk from the ground, and became a main stand season ticket holder. Taken into the Vice Presidents Club by his boss, VPC founder Bill Bouttell, in 1970, he has been there ever since, serving in various capacities. In 1973 a crisis at Radio Addenbrookes led to him being handed the microphone at half time. Later that evening attempts to prise it out of his hands were successful. He subsequently became their match commentator until commentaries to hospitals were superseded in the 1980s by the advent of local radio. Recruited by Chiltern Radio, he became their voice at the Abbey until the station stopped broadcasting sports and news shows in the mid-1990s. Graham is a retired industrial safety officer. His two sons, Richard and Owen, are fanatical Cambridge United supporters in their adopted homes of Teesside and the United States. He lists his sporting career highlights as playing for Mayfield School PTA against a side that included Terry Eades, and scoring 83 not out in the Civil Service Cup final on Parkers Piece, on a pitch prepared by former Cambridge United goalie, Arthur Morgan.

Introduction

When we first came together to undertake this book, we little realised what a time consuming yet fascinating project this was to be. We started with the advantage of having both been full-time supporters for over thirty-five years and had witnessed at first hand nearly half the history of the club through being actively involved in various supporters' organisations. Strangely though, between us we only had a handful of photographs.

Fortunately, we both agreed very early on the events, games, personalities and players we wanted to be commemorated in this book. In every football club there are milestones and people that change the future. At Cambridge these included moving to the Abbey Stadium in the 1930s, the founding of the Supporters Club in 1947 and the Vice Presidents Club in 1969, and the change of name from Abbey United to Cambridge United. In the 1950s the first shares were issued, the club moved towards professional status, ex-international players Wilf Mannion, Sam McCrory and Brian Moore were signed, and improvements to the ground started. After joining the Southern League, the determined and professional approach of Geoff Proctor and the Board built the best non-League club in Britain, resulting in election to the Football League in 1970. We wanted to record those early League managers who built the success – Bill Leivers, Ron Atkinson, and John Docherty, the slump of the mid-1980s and the arrival of Chris Turner. The John Beck years brought heady excitement, including two successive quarter-final appearances in the FA Cup, an appearance at Wembley and the play-offs to join the Premiership. Nobody liked us but we did not care. There were the ups and downs of the 1990s and at last, after nearly twenty-five years, getting planning permission to redevelop the stadium over the next few years. We have managed to cover them all and more, thanks to some outstanding help and co-operation from a number of people and organisations.

Both photographic and written material from the early years is very thin on the ground. Before the Second World War, Abbey United, as they were called then, were only on a par with the better village and works teams. A photographer or reporter was only likely to turn up during a cup run or a crunch game. Fortunately United always seemed to do well in the local competition, the Creake Shield. The turning point came in 1951 when the club changed its name to Cambridge United after turning semi-professional, and that is when they started to become a major force. It was not until 1952 that Cambridge United recorded their first victory over Cambridge City, or 'Town' as they were known until Cambridge became a city in 1951. The progress then made – in under twenty years – to achieve Football League status was little short of a miracle and to find the club on the very edge of the joining the Premiership, arguably the top league in the world, just twenty more years later, is a tribute to everyone involved – directors, managers, players and fans alike. The fact that Cambridge United has never had that cradle of large scale support – a local industrial base – to draw on makes the club's achievements all the more remarkable.

We have tried to make this a book for all fans produced by two fans. This club has only existed for just over eighty years, and there are still supporters around who were born before the club was. Nevertheless, the history has been a fascinating one and the contribution made by the club has greatly enriched the life of the Abbey Ward and Cambridge. We hope that in some small way we have been able to preserve some of that history and pay tribute to some of the people who have made Cambridge United what it is.

Brian Attmore and Graham Nurse
June 2001

Acknowledgements

The bulk of the pictures we have used have come from four sources. Without any one of them, this book could not have been compiled. Colin Grant, editor of the *Cambridge Evening News*, has given us an enormous amount of co-operation, even lending us vital negatives from the paper's archives where prints were not available. He and his staff have shown us nothing but helpfulness, and underlined the commitment of the *Cambridge Evening News* to Cambridge United and the community. The photographs of the very early years have been placed for some time in the Cambridgeshire Collection, the community archives of the history of Cambridge, and without their help and co-operation in tracking material down, and reproducing it, we never could have achieved the completeness we have aimed for. Two people have provided almost all the photographs of the 1990s. Dave Smith, a life-long fan and club photographer, produced thousands of images of that era, including the memorable cup runs and the Wembley play-offs, all of which he made freely available to us. When it came to the late 1990s, the club's public relations manager, Graham Eales, allowed us access to photographs he had taken for the programme, as well as many of his personal photographs. As a result of both his and Dave Smith's help, we were able to use some exceptional and humorous images that have never been printed before.

There are many other people who have helped us, either by finding material or answering our appeals for their photographs, and we gratefully acknowledge their help and support with this project. They are: John Abbott, Elaine Ballinger, Dave Brown, Alan Burge, Kate Burrell (the daughter of ex-chairman Geoffrey Proctor), Sandra Burton, John Cash, Martin Chapman, Ray Clarke, Colin Davies, Dick Dunn, Tom Gurney, Martin Langford, Carol Looker, Dave Matthews-Jones, Ann Miles and the Cambridge Camera Club, Brian Moore, Kevan Murphy, Ralph Newbrook, Nigel Pearce, Terry Pink, Colin Purdew, Jolyon Rea, Taff Rees, Rodney Slack, Reg Smart, David Stroud, Andrea Thrussell and Herald Express Publications for permission to use their photograph of the team arriving at Torquay in 1954. Without all these people, and the patience and support of our wives, Pamela and Janet, our task would have been so much harder.

Most of the research has been done by ourselves and from our own records, in particular Graham's written accounts of every match played since the late 1980s. Nevertheless, three books have been our constant companions during the project – *United in Endeavour* and *On the Up* by Paul Daw and *Cambridge United: The League Era* by Kevin Palmer. These have allowed us to add background information and attribute certain photographs to an exact date, which would not have been possible without hours of further research. In particular we would like to thank Paul Daw for access to material he researched but did not include in his books.

To all these people, and any others that we may have inadvertently left out, we extend our grateful thanks. We have been, in the words of the club's motto, 'United in Endeavour'.

One
The Early Days
1912-40

A club called Cambridge United was formed in 1908. Later, in 1912, some young men from the Abbey Ward got together to form a team they called Abbey United, who played their first recorded game against M.J. Drew's XI on 22 November 1913. Both teams were disbanded at the outbreak of the First World War. When those who came back from the fighting returned to Cambridge, Abbey United was reformed but not Cambridge United. The club remained Abbey United until 1951 when it was re-named Cambridge United. This photograph shows the players and officials of the original 'Cambridge United' club of 1912.

Abbey United shared the Creake Charity Shield with United Cantabs in the 1924/25 season. From left to right, back row: Bill Walker, Harvey Cornwell, C.E. Elsden, Percy Wilson, -?-, Harold Watson, Fanny Freeman, Tom Bilton. Middle row: H. Bowman, Jim Self, -?-, George Alsop, Bob Patman, Pimp Stearn, William Taverner. Front row: H.F. Newman, Charlie Taverner.

In 1926/27 the team were runners-up in the Cambs League. From left to right, back row: C. Morley, Fred Stevens, Joe Livermore, F. Clements, Harvey Cornwell, Harold Watson. Front row (sitting): Dick Harris, Edward Fuller, George Alsop, C. Clements, William Walker. Now playing in black and amber stripes, the team had been nicknamed 'The Wasps'.

ABBEY UNITED FOOTBALL CLUB.

Hon. Sec.—G. W. CHAPMAN, 64, VINERY ROAD, CAMBRIDGE.

....19

Dear Sir,
      You are selected to play for the above Club against
....at..

on Saturday.......................... Kick off at..........................
If unable to play, please notify.

      The team will travel by..

from..

        G. W· CHAPMAN, *Hon. Secretary.*

In the early days of Abbey United, a selection committee met mid-week to pick the side. The secretary, George Chapman, then cycled to each player's house to deliver a completed version of the above card. If nothing further was heard, it was assumed that the player would turn up.

The Bury Cup, Cambs Challenge Cup, Creake Shield, Cambs League Division One Cup and the Chatteris Cup were all won by Abbey United in 1929. From left to right, back row: H. Bowman, Jack Rayner, William Walker, F. Clements, Harold Watson, George Chapman, Tom Bilton. Middle row: Cyril Haylock, Dick Harris, George Alsop, Henry Clement Francis, Harvey Cornwell, Bob Patman. Front row: Sid Hulyer, T. James.

At Milton Road on 28 April 1928, Abbey United lost 2-0 to Cambridge Town Reserves in the final of the Creake Shield. The following Saturday they beat Romsey Town 3-0 to win the Chatteris Engineering Works Cup.

'32-3	1st ELEVEN.	GR'ND	Result f. a.				1932-3.	2nd ELEVEN.	GR'ND	R. f.
pt. 3	F.A. Cup, Histon	home					Sept 24	Girton	away	
10	Linton	home					Oct. 1	Minor Cup P.R., Girton	home	
17	Soham R.	away					8			
24	Gamlingay	home					15	Minor Cup, 1st Round.		
t. 1							22	Cottenham	home	
8	Histon	away					29	Granchester	away	
15	Ely City	home					Nov. 5	Minor Cup, 2nd Rd., Orwell	home	
22	Linton	away					12	Sawson P.M. Res.	away	
29	Sawston P.M.	home					19	Newnham Inst.	away	
ov. 5	R.A.F. Duxford	away					26	Girton	home	
12	Pye Radio, Challenge Cup, 2nd Rd.	away					Dec. 3	Coton	home	
19	Soham R.	home					10			
26	Ely City	away					17	Fulbourn	away	
ec. 3	Challenge Cup, 3rd Rd.						24			
10	Royeston	home					B.D. 26			
17	R.A.F. Duxford	home					31			
24	Swifts, Charity Shield, 1st Rd.	away					Jan. 7	Sawson P.M. Res.	home	
.D. 26							14	Royston Res.	home	
31	Uni. Press	home					21			
n. 2							28			
7							Feb. 4			
14							11	Orwell	away	
21	Charity Shield, 2nd Rd.						18	Sawston Inst.	away	
28	Uni. Press	away					25	Fulbourn	home	
eb. 4	Gamlingay	away					Mar. 4	Sawston Inst.	home	
11	Charity Shield, 3rd Rd.						11	Granchester	ho ne	
18	Histon	home					18	Coton	away	
25	Royeston	away					25	Cottenham	away	
ar. 4	Sawston P.M.	away					April 1	Royston Res.	away	
11	U. Cantabs.	away					8	Newnham Inst.	home	
18							15			
25	U. Cantabs.	home					22			
pril 1	Swifts	home					29			
8										
15										
22										
29										

MEMBER'S CARD.

SEASON'S RECORD. — Won — Lost — Drawn

The fixture list for 1932/33 – the season Abbey United moved to the Abbey Stadium – was produced in an imitation blue leather cover with gold lettering. The club headquarters are given as the Dog & Pheasant in Newmarket Road.

A monumental day in the club's history came on 31 August 1932 with the opening of the Abbey Stadium. Built on land purchased by its president, Henry Clement Francis, it was opened by his daughter, Mrs K. Saxon. There followed a friendly fixture in which University Press were beaten 2-0 with both goals scored by Jackie Bond.

The inaugural competitive match at the Abbey saw a 5-4 defeat by Histon Institute in the FA Cup on 3 September 1932. The first goal came from Harvey Cornwell. Here, the Abbey United goalkeeper is seen in action during the tie.

Not only did the president, H.C. Francis, provide the Abbey Stadium for the club, he also gave the first stand. It was opened on 10 March 1934 when Abbey United beat Gamlingay 1-0 with a goal by Fred Tavener.

Coton Institute were thrashed 7-2 in the Creake Shield on 10 February 1934. Here, the Coton goalkeeper is making a brave attempt, but cannot stop United's third goal. Three weeks later Coton came from behind to get a 2-2 draw with United, the point giving them the Cambs Premier League title which would otherwise have gone to United.

In the 1934 Creake Shield final, United beat Pye Radio 3-2 after extra time, with two goals from Harvey Cornwell and one from 'Darley' Watson. From left to right, back row: Charlie Taverner, Bob Brown, Harry Wilsher, Harvey Cornwell, William Asplin, Fred Taverner. Front row: Fred Bowles, Harold 'Darley' Watson, Wally Wilson, Herbert Bailey, Jackie Bond.

No goalie worth his salt in the 1930s went without a good pair of gloves and a large cap. This action comes from the Creake Shield semi-final, which was held at Cambridge Town's Milton Road ground on 28 March 1936. Abbey United beat Sawston Church Institute 4-0 with two goals from Fred Sewell, and one each for Basil Saunders and Harvey Cornwell. They went on to beat Coton Institute in the final.

In the final of the Creake Shield on 22 April 1936, Coton were beaten 2-1. From left to right, back row: Harry Wilsher, Wally Wilson, Reg Kimberley, Fred Sewell, Jim Langford, Len Johnson. Front row: Harvey Cornwell, Basil Saunders, William Asplen, Fred Tavener, Ernie Wilsher.

Abbey United won the Creake Shield in 1939 with a 2-1 victory over Histon Institute, watched by 1,200 spectators. Both goals were scored by centre forward Herbert Smart, father of the future chairman, Reg Smart. From left to right, back row: Herbert Smart, Reg Kimberley, Buck Arnold, Ron Sanderson, Ernie Caston, Reg Wilson. Front row: Fred Mansfield, Monty Bull, Wally Wilson, Bob Brown, Joe Richardson, Jim Langford.

Two
Planting the Seeds of Ambition
1940-60

After the Second World War, the Abbey Stadium became one of the focal points of life in the Abbey area of the city. Regular fetes, and even a gymkhana and a celebration organised by the American Forces, were held at the ground in the close season. This is believed to be an event held at the Abbey in the early 1950s – which is likely to have been one of the following: celebrations following Cambridge being given city status, the Labour Day celebrations organised by Romsey Labour Club, or the Coronation Party in 1953.

The Supporters Club was founded on 2 October 1947. The management committee in 1954 consisted of, from left to right, back row: J. Blackwell, R. Clifford, E. Ward, D. Grant, H. Brown. Front row: Jenny Morgan, Bill Harrison, Harry Habbin, Percy Neal, Lil Harrison.

A dinner for the Abbey United Supporters Club was held on 6 May 1950 in the Burleigh Street Co-op Rooms. From left to right: Mrs Habbin, Mrs Covill, Tom Gurney, Mr H. Barrance, and the vicar of Christchurch, Newmarket Road. Tom Gurney, later a founder member of the Vice Presidents Club, and Mr Barrance, a solicitor who was the club's auditor, were members of the fund-raising committee that preceded the Supporters Club and met in the Globe opposite the ground.

The Supporters Club members were given a badge when they joined. In 1962, to help fund the upgrade of the floodlights, a popular badge was produced which sold at the not inconsiderable sum of £1.

A record crowd of 5,000 were at the Abbey on 17 January 1948 for the first round proper of the FA Amateur Cup. Captain Joe Richardson (on the right) is pictured greeting the Cambridge Town captain. Town were 1-0 victors in a close encounter.

'Mr Cambridge United' Geoffrey Proctor was the outstanding director and chairman in the history of the club. He served as vice-chairman from 1950 to 1954, chairman from 1954 to 1961, and then director from 1961 until his death in 1974, having taken over the chair again six months previously on the death of the former incumbent, John Woolley. He is recognised as the man whose vision and tenacity resulted in the election of Cambridge United to the Football League in 1970. The boardroom at Cambridge United is named after him.

Mo. 15   *Five* **Shares.**

ABBEY UNITED FOOTBALL CLUB (CAMBRIDGE)

LIMITED.

(Incorporated under the Companies Act, 1948.)

CAPITAL   -   -   -   £5,000

Divided into 400 "A" Shares of £10 each, and 2,000 "B" Shares of 10/- each.

This is to Certify that *Mr Geoffrey Charles Proctor* of *64, Newmarket Road, Cambridge* ——————— is the Registered Proprietor of *Five* ——————— "A" Shares of £10 each, FULLY PAID, numbered *106* to *110* inclusive, in **ABBEY UNITED FOOTBALL CLUB (CAMBRIDGE) LIMITED,** pursuant to the Memorandum and Articles of Association of the said Company.

Given under the Common Seal of the Company this *21st* day of *December* 1950

S. V. Starr
Wmaclaren Francis } DIRECTORS.
N. A. Barker SECRETARY.

An ambitious Abbey United first issued shares in the football club in 1950. This is share certificate number 15, issued to Geoffrey Proctor, and one of several share purchases he made on behalf of himself and members of his family. It is signed by the chairman, W. Maclaren Francis, and the director, Stan Starr.

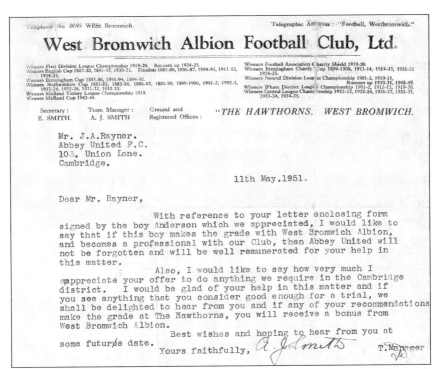

Secretary :　　　Team Manager :　　Ground and　　　　"THE HAWTHORNS, WEST BROMWICH.
E. SMITH.　　　A. J. SMITH.　　Registered Offices :

　　　　Mr. J.A.Rayner.
　　　　Abbey United F.C.
　　　　103. Union Lane.
　　　　Cambridge.

　　　　　　　　　　　　　　11th May.1951.

　　　　Dear Mr. Rayner,

　　　　　　　With reference to your letter enclosing form
signed by the boy Anderson which we appreciated, I would like to
say that if this boy makes the grade with West Bromwich Albion,
and becomes a professional with our Club, then Abbey United will
not be forgotten and will be well remunerated for your help in
this matter.
　　　　　　　Also, I would like to say how very much I
appreciate your offer to do anything we require in the Cambridge
district.　I would be glad of your help in this matter and if
you see anything that you consider good enough for a trial, we
shall be delighted to hear from you and if any of your recommendations
make the grade at The Hawthorns, you will receive a bonus from
West Bromwich Albion.
　　　　　　　Best wishes and hoping to hear from you at
some future date.
　　　　　　Yours faithfully,　A. J. Smith　　　T. Manager

The club made one of their first transfers of a local player to a major League club in 1951, when Percy Anderson went to West Bromwich Albion. He was later to return to the club after playing for West Brom and Stockport.

The first game in the Eastern Counties League as the renamed Cambridge United was on 18 August 1951. The newly completed Supporters Club, built by volunteers, is in the background with the trees that stood outside the ground entrance. From left to right, back row: Albert George, Bill Whittaker (player-manager), Henry Bullen, John Percival, Tony Gallego, Bob Bishop, Jack Thomas, Reg Barker (trainer). Front row: Stan Thurston, Russell Crane, Ray Ruffett, Len Crowe, Joe Gallego.

Cambridge United won the Cambs Invitation Cup in 1952 with a 2-0 victory over Cambridge City at their Milton Road ground. The mayor, Alderman H. Langdon, presented the trophy to United's captain, Ray Ruffett. It was the first victory over Cambridge City in a competitive match, with both goals scored by Russell Crane.

The first ever game against League opposition was in November 1953 in the FA Cup. After a 2-2 draw with Newport County at the Abbey, watched by 7,500, United recorded an astonishing giant-killing 2-1 victory in Wales, with goals from Len Saward and Les Stevens. Arthur Morgan is shown collecting the ball at Newport, watched by Russell Crane in the centre.

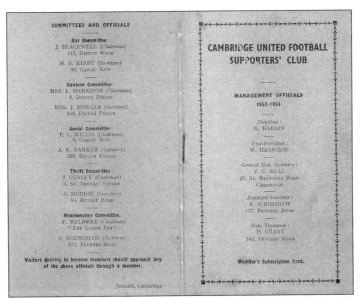

The Supporters Clubhouse was built in 1951 by volunteer labour organised by Geoffrey Proctor. Its popularity with non-members led to the introduction of a visitor's fee of three pence per visit. The annual subscription in 1953/54 was five shillings (the price of twenty visitor's daily charges).

The 1953/54 Eastern Counties League campaign started with 10 games without a defeat. United eventually finished in third place, behind King's Lynn and Clacton. From left to right, back row: Reg Barker (trainer), Bob Bishop, Len Saward, Johnnie Percival, Albert George, Arthur Morgan. Front row: Teddy Bowd, Len Crowe, Bill Whittaker (player-manager), Ray Ruffett (captain), Russell Crane, Les Stevens.

Cambridge United got through to the first round of the FA Cup for the second year running in 1954. They were met at Torquay station by the Torquay chairman and manager. The unmistakable giant figure of Cambridge chairman Geoff Proctor is in the middle of this photograph. Ron Thulbourn, the director who was landlord of the Rose and Crown in Teversham, stands to the left holding his mackintosh.

Player-manager Bill Whittaker lays down the tactics in the dressing room before the game. Listening to him, from left to right, are: Bob Bishop, Teddy Bowd, Peter Dobson, Harry Bullen, Len Crowe, Russell Crane, Arthur Morgan, Jack Thomas and Percy Anderson. There was to be no repeat of last season's giant-killing and 8,224 saw Torquay run out easy 4-0 winners.

The third or 'A' team of several big clubs played in the Eastern Counties League. A packed Newmarket Road end watches the game against Spurs 'A' on Easter Monday 1954. At the end of this season, volunteers built the terracing and walls for the Newmarket Road end stand, with contractors fitting the roof in October.

Arsenal 'A' were also regular visitors to the Abbey. This action photograph from 1954 shows Len Crowe and Les Stevens chasing down the Arsenal 'keeper. The 'A' teams of Arsenal, Spurs, West Ham and Norwich all finished below United at the end of this campaign.

With fans sitting on the touchline so close that their feet are on the pitch, Len Saward goes close at the Allotments End in 1956. That season Ely City put United out of the FA Cup, winning 5-2 at the Abbey.

Russell Crane was given a benefit match in April 1956 when his Select XI and a Combined XI drew 2-2 in front of 1,500 fans. Here, he introduces the mayoress to his team-mates. The previous December had seen United's first ever game under floodlights.

In the summer of 1956 came the sensational signing of the legendary Wilf Mannion, who had been banned from League football after his newspaper allegations of 'under the counter' payments. He is shown here skipping past a challenge during his first game in August 1956. In the background are the changing rooms, which were near the half-way line in what is now the Habbin Stand.

The team for that first match of the 1956/57 season. From left to right, back row: Russell Crane, Ron Murchison, Harry Chapman, Ted Culver, Johnny Strachan, Bert Johnson (player-manager). Front row: Brian Iley, Wilf Mannion, Ian McPherson, Len Saward, Kevin Barry. The mascot was John Dunn. United beat Bury 5-3 on this occasion.

On Easter Monday 1957, a crowd of 9,668 watched United beat Cambridge City 1-0 at Milton Road to win the Cambs Invitation Cup. From left to right, back row: Len Saward, Bernard Moore, Colin Senior, Ted Culver, Harry Chapman, Jock Kyle, Bob Bishop. Front row: Russell Crane, Brian Moore, Ron Murchison, Wilf Mannion, Kevin Barry. The mascot was John Dunn.

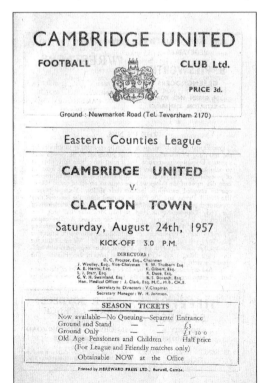

The last-ever season in the Eastern Counties League started on 24 August 1957. Cambridge United ended the season runners-up to Tottenham Hotspur 'A' and their application to join the Southern League was accepted. Note the price of season tickets – ground and stand £3, ground only £1-10-0, old age pensioners and children half price.

Right: Cambridge United gave Wilf Mannion two benefit matches in 1958 against All Star teams. In March, 9,500 fans saw a team of internationals comprised of: Ted Ditchburn, Lawrie Scott, Jack Howe, Henry Cockburn, Neil Franklin, Joe Mercer, Derek Tapscott, Jimmy Hagan, Stan Mortenson, Johnny Morris and Bobby Langton. A month later some of them returned, and were joined by Wally Barnes, Alf Sherwood, Eddie Boot, Willie Watson, Willie Moir, Jimmy Hagan, Peter Doherty and Charlie Mitten. This photograph was taken before that second game. On the right of the front row are the two Cambridge United ex-internationals – Wilf Mannion and Brian Moore. The referee is Jack Cooke, who was later to become a Cambridge United director.

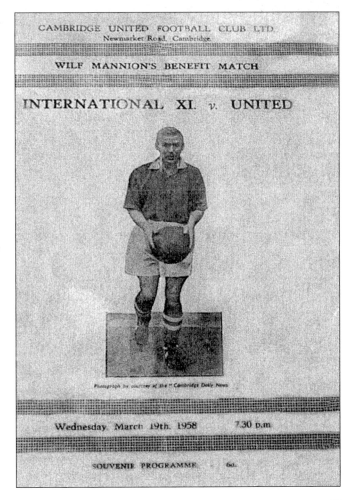

CAMBRIDGE UNITED FOOTBALL CLUB LTD.
Newmarket Road, Cambridge.

WILF MANNION'S BENEFIT MATCH

INTERNATIONAL XI *v.* UNITED

Photograph by courtesy of the "Cambridge Daily News"

Wednesday, March 19th, 1958   7.30 p.m.

SOUVENIR PROGRAMME   6d.

Brian Moore joined Cambridge United in December 1956 to play alongside his boyhood hero, Wilf Mannion. Forced out of top-flight football at the age of twenty-two by an eye injury which partially blinded him, the ex-West Ham and Ireland international scored a record-breaking 68 goals in the 1957/58 season. Wilf Mannion considered this goal to be the best.

During the 1957/58 season, the first floodlights were installed on surplus telegraph poles. Brian Moore is shown adding to his tally at the Allotments End with a typically clinical finish. United ended the season as Eastern Counties League runners-up to Spurs 'A'.

Manager Bert Johnson (extreme right) with two Charlton players, presenting Brian Moore with an inscribed ball to mark his 68 goals during the 1957/58 season. The ball credits him with only 64 goals.

Directors, staff and their wives join Brian Moore at the dinner held to mark his achievement. From left to right: Bert Johnson (manager), Paddy Harris, Ron Thulbourn, Tony Dosangh, John Woolley, Jack Abblet (Cambs FA), Percy Neal (Supporters Club), Vic Chapman (secretary).

Frank Lock, followed by Taffy Jones, Jock Campbell and Alan Bull, leaving the old dressing rooms by the Cut Throat Lane entrance in 1957. The rooms were later converted into the lottery office and the cash room before becoming toilets.

Youth teams were entered in both sections of the Cambs Youth League in the 1958/59 season and both won their sections with 100 per cent records. From left to right, back row: John Cash, Robin Caston, Roger ?, Tim Langran, Tony Wilson, Reg Tailby, Vic Phillips, Roger Hart, Roger Smith. Front row: -?-, Alan Carter, Graham Ward, Bob Dellar, Johnny Munns, Dave Stocker, John Humpries, ? Wilson, Roger Wisbey. Tailby, Hart and Ward progressed to the first team, with Hart and Ward playing League football with West Brom and Watford respectively.

Three

The Best Non-Leaguers in the Land

1960-70

In the mid-1960s, Cambridge United and Cambridge City met up to six times a season in various competitions. In this action shot, Rodney Slack saves at the Coldhams Common end in the January 1965 Southern League game.

Fans on the railway sleeper terraces watch as Alan Moore, partially hidden by the goal post, sends the ball right across the face of the Corby goal in the 2-0 victory on Boxing Day 1959. The ex-Sunderland and Nottingham Forest player had been appointed player-coach a fortnight earlier and was made player-manager in February 1960.

Alan Moore, manager from 1960 to 1963, was responsible for the far-reaching decision to make all of the first team full-time professionals in 1960. Here he is seen in jovial mood with directors and fellow smokers Matt Wynn and Sam Tanner.

The Habbin Stand, named after Harry Habbin, the first chairman of the Supporters Club, was completed and new floodlights ordered during the 1962/63 season. Matt McVittie heads towards the allotments end goal during that season with the old stand, tea bar and terrace of raised railway sleepers in the background. The redevelopment of that side of the ground was still in the planning stage.

The Southern League Cup was won for the first time in April 1962. After a 2-2 home draw in the first leg with goals from Billy Welsh and Roy Kirk, they won the away leg at Margate 2-1. An own goal and one from Mike Dixon brought the Cup to the Abbey.

The 1964/65 season was the heaviest ever for the first team, who played no fewer than 91 games, winning 46 and drawing 18. Seen boarding the coach for the FA Cup match at Barnet in November 1964 are, from left to right: Brian Boggis, Rodney Slack, Jimmy Gibson, John Haasz, Matt McVittie, Derek Finch, Billy Day.

Roy Kirk starts a training session on Coldhams Common in 1965 with press-ups. The popular Kirk was manager from 1963 to 1966, when he resigned, which led to the appointment of Bill Leivers in February 1967, with Kirk as his coach.

The fans' hero of the 1960s was Rodney Slack. Here, he is shown collecting the ball as Cambridge City's Eddie Bailham spins away in disbelief in 1965. The previous year, Bailham played for his country against England when he was at Shamrock Rovers. Significantly, Rodney Slack and Cambridge United were to cross swords with him again when he was leading goalscorer for arch-rivals Wimbledon in the late 1960s.

After being voted player of the season three times in his first five years at the Abbey, the Board awarded Rodney Slack a benefit game in 1966. A crowd of 4,000 turned up to watch a game against the cast of the BBC TV series *United*.

The bitter rivalry between Cambridge United and Cambridge City spilt over at the Newmarket Road end when the teams met in this game in April 1965. Three years after the incident shown here, referee Scotty Denson, himself an experienced ex-player, was forced to abandon a game between the two sides when fighting on the pitch led to spectators joining in. Both clubs were severely censured.

Matt McVittie was transferred to Cambridge City in the summer of 1965. His first game for them, that August, was against his former colleagues. Rodney Slack watches anxiously as City's Alan Gregory, scorer of the game's only goal, shoots wide.

The leading goalscorer for two consecutive seasons, Peter Hobbs, challenges the Weymouth goalkeeper in March 1966. He scored the only goal of this encounter. The new stand had been used for the first time on 21 February of this year.

Peter Hobbs was the match ball sponsor twenty-six years later for the game against Stoke in 1992. Here, he hands the ball to Lee Philpott.

As the referee calms the players down, Rodney Slack is being stretchered off following a bad challenge at Hereford in 1966. Their player-manager, John Charles, wisely left the perpetrator out of the return match at the Abbey later that season.

Despite two mid-table finishes in the mid-1960s, United joined Wigan as highest losers in the Football League re-election ballots. In December 1966, two goals from Dave Bennett and one from Wes Maughan claimed the points at Worcester, where traditionally a photograph was taken. From left to right, back row: Colin Toon, Rodney Slack, Jackie Scurr, John Turley, Gerry Graham, Gerry Baker. Front row: Mike Fairchild, Wesley Maughan, Peter Hobbs, Alan O'Neill, David Bennett.

Matches against Chelmsford were always closely contested. Here, a Chelmsford defender clears in a game during the 1966/67 season. In 1966, both Chelmsford and Cambridge City were eliminated from the Football League elections because they had signed League players without the League's consent, effectively ending their quests for League status.

Here, Colin Toon heads clear in the match at Chelmsford in the 1966/67 season. Both sides ended the season on the same points, with Romford claiming the title.

In the days before safety barriers, fans sat on the wall in front of the Habbin stand, right on the touchline. They are watching Alan O'Neill in action during the 1967/68 season.

Cambridge finished third in the Southern League in May 1968. Here, David Chambers, Billy Wall and Jackie Scurr celebrate number nine, Ian Hutchinson's equaliser in the April draw at Wimbledon – who finished the season as runners-up. The following season, when Cambridge United did the Southern League Championship and Cup double, twenty-four coaches left the Supporters Club car park for the crunch match at Plough Lane.

'Cambridge United' was the racehorse bought by a syndicate of the directors to run in black and amber colours and publicise the drive to get elected to the Football League.

Former reserve team trainer Ron Simpson was struck down by illness and confined to a wheelchair in 1967. Ex-United and ex-City players teamed up for a benefit match for him. Among the United players dusting off their boots after many years were Ron Murchison, Neville Brown, Taffy Jones, Keith Payne, Roy Kirk, Frank Lock, Reg Pearce, Bill Heath, Russell Crane (twenty-six years after his debut) and Alan Moore.

The match against Chelsea, which was part of the Ian Hutchinson transfer deal, attracted the largest crowd ever seen at the Abbey Stadium. With Cambridge facing the Southern League Championship decider the following day, 14,000 fans saw Chelsea Reserves replace United for the second half.

Chelsea paraded the FA Cup they had won earlier that week in the replay against Leeds. Cambridge secretary Phil Baker is seen in the background as the St John's ambulance volunteers count the proceeds of the collection. This was taken in the traditional way, the fans throwing their loose change into a blanket carried round the ground.

In the days before the Coldham's Common end became the terrace for the away fans, many of the regulars watched from that vantage point. Few seemed unworried about being sitting targets with a twelve foot drop into the allotments behind them, should a wayward shot head their way.

Nine of the FA Cup-winning side played in the highly entertaining match against Chelsea. The Blues led 1-0 at half time but were finally beaten 4-3 after an impressive display by their second string players, who replaced United in the second half. From left to right: Tommy Baldwin, Peter Houseman, John Dempsey, Ron Harris.

Ian Hutchinson watches Rodney Slack, in his penultimate appearance, claim the ball from number seven, Tommy Baldwin.

The final non-League game was on 2 May 1970. After clinching the Southern League title with a 2-0 victory over Margate, who had formed a guard of honour to applaud them onto the pitch, the players paraded the championship trophy for the second season running.

Manager Bill Leivers gives the thumbs up at Heathrow on 29 May 1970 as he and the players depart for a tour of Germany. The following day Cambridge United were elected to the Football League with 31 votes. Their main opponents, Bradford Park Avenue, had only managed 17.

The dream came true on 30 May 1970 – club social organiser Bill Pink celebrates election to the Football League. (In those days, Peterborough was not in Cambridgeshire.)

Four

Into the League
1970-74

It was a royal reception when Cambridge United paraded down Kings Parade in June 1970. The team coach, bringing them home from the airport after the tour of Germany, had been met at Royston by their families, friends and fans. On arrival on the outskirts of Cambridge, they were led in triumph to a civic reception at the Guildhall to mark their election to the Football League.

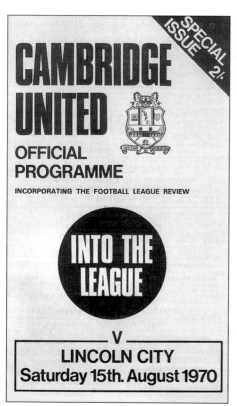

SPECIAL ISSUE 2/-

CAMBRIDGE UNITED

OFFICIAL PROGRAMME

INCORPORATING THE FOOTBALL LEAGUE REVIEW

INTO THE LEAGUE

V

LINCOLN CITY
Saturday 15th. August 1970

The first ever game in the Football League at the Abbey Stadium attracted a gate of 6,843. Lincoln took the lead after just eight minutes with a goal from Derek Travis, the move having been begun by future England manager Graham Taylor.

After Lincoln had seen three efforts cleared off the line, the first goal scored by Cambridge United in the League came after seventy-eight minutes of football. Colin Meldrum leaps above the defence to power home John McKinven's corner to earn the point.

Cambridge United chairman John Woolley opened the new extension to the Supporters Club in the summer of 1971. On his left is Lil Harrison, stalwart of the Supporters Club Committee, and on his right the Supporters Club secretary, John Spence, and chairman, Les Selmes.

On his home debut, Brian Greenhalgh (left) and Ivan Hollett watch as Miss Cambridge United, seventeen-year-old Julie Owen, kicks off the 1971/72 season at the Abbey. Chris Foote was the scorer in the 1-1 draw with Northampton that day. Julie was the daughter of tireless United workers Charlie and Glad Owen.

In the first ever game in the Midweek League in August 1971, George Harris collected a kick from Charlton's Dave Shipperley which was enough to make all the men in the 1,700 crowd wince at the same time. Fortunately, no lasting damage was done.

United learnt the hard way when they played Second Division opponents for the first time. Fulham won 4-0 at Craven Cottage in the League Cup in 1971 with Malcolm Webster, later to make 256 League appearances for Cambridge, their goalkeeper that day. Here he is under challenge from Vic Akers, with Brian Greenhalgh, John Collins and Chris Foote watching in the background.

As Cambridge United found their feet in the Football League, they finished in tenth place at the conclusion of the 1971/72 season. This was due in no small part to arrival of Brian Greenhalgh, pictured here challenging for a cross in the final game against Scunthorpe. United won 2-0, with Greenhalgh scoring his nineteenth goal of the season.

Trevor Roberts was the fearless goalkeeper Bill Leivers signed on election to the Football League. Six weeks into the season he developed a mysterious chest infection, which was diagnosed as lung cancer. Incredibly, he was back in the side by April, but within a year he was cruelly struck down by a stroke and a reoccurrence of the disease. He is seen here in the dressing room at his testimonial in May 1972 against West Ham. Roberts died later that year.

The first promotion came on 28 April 1973, when 11,542 crammed into the Abbey for the game against Mansfield. Whoever won would be promoted, with the losers staying down. Fans on top of the old Tannoy box are watching as the 'keeper punches a corner under challenge from David Lill, with Brian Greenhalgh hoping the ball will drop to him.

Twice Cambridge came from behind with goals from Ronnie Walton and Bobby Ross. Then the Abbey erupted as Walton drove home this goal to give Cambridge the 3-2 win.

A Vice Presidents Club had been formed in 1969, with director Paddy Harris as chairman. In the summer of 1973, VPC founder and secretary Bill Bouttell, and committee members Stan Cutter and Graham Nurse, built a new box with upgraded seating for the first Third Division campaign. When the stand was rebuilt in 1980, the VPC members turned the bare shell of a room into the Harris Suite.

The team photograph for the first-ever season in Third Division, 1973/74, did not show Bobby Ross (scorer of the first United goal in that division), and Dave Lennard (who was signed that summer). The step up in class proved too much for the side, however, and Cambridge went straight back to the Fourth Division. From left to right, back row: Freeman, Bannister, Foote, Lill, Eades, Guild, Rathbone, Ferguson, O'Donnell. Front row: Smith, Greenhalgh, Simmonds, Akers, Harris, Vasper.

As the 1973/74 relegation season came to an end, full-back Vic Akers wore the number eleven shirt to play as an emergency striker. He scored twice – including a spectacular back-headed goal – in the 3-1 victory over Plymouth, which was watched by the smallest Abbey crowd for eight years. Akers later became manager of Arsenal FC Ladies.

Cambridge United staged the first professional football match played on a Sunday. On 6 January 1974 they drew 2-2 with Oldham in the FA Cup. The game kicked off at 10.45 due to floodlight restrictions during the three-day working week, with admittance by programme, as taking money at the gate was illegal. Here, Dave Simmonds pressurises Ian Woods into an own goal.

Five

Mr Bojangles and
The Doc
1974-83

For nine heady years, first Ron Atkinson and then John Docherty built teams to take and keep the club in the old Second Division. Celebrating promotion to the Second Division on 29 April 1978 are, from left to right: Alan Biley, Gordon Sweetzer, Sammy Morgan (partially hidden), vice chairman Tony Douglas (who has a special word of congratulation for Biley), Dr Clark (the club physician), Dave Stringer, Tom Finney, Steve Spriggs and Lindsay Smith. Chairman David Rushton is standing behind Dave Stringer.

In December 1974, Ron Atkinson, manager of Kettering Town, was appointed after the sacking of Bill Leivers. With his gold jewellery, the press christened the flamboyant new boss 'Mr Bojangles'. His baptism of fire was a 1-0 victory at Stockport, with Brendon Batson sent off for punching an opponent – after what Atkinson alleged was a racist remark – goalkeeper Graham Smith injured after 30 minutes and captain Nigel Cassidy collecting eight stitches in a facial wound.

In under three months Ron Atkinson took the side from sixteenth place to sixth. Here, Graham Watson scores after three minutes against Crewe in April 1975. Three minutes later, Tommy Horsfall made it 2-0.

By the final home match in the season he arrived, Ron Atkinson's record was impressive – won 13, drawn 6, lost 2 – and promotion was missed by just 3 points. Leading scorer Bobby Shinton, watched by Tommy Horsfall, is pictured going close in the 2-0 victory over Scunthorpe.

With money short, Ron Atkinson signed discarded teenagers Steve Spriggs from Huddersfield and Alan Biley from Luton in the summer of 1975. The two, who were to become Cambridge United legends, are being greeted by captain Terry Eades (seen on the left). The youngster between them is recorded as 'R. Bryant' – whatever happened to him?

After 2 goals in his first 2 games, Alan Biley broke his leg at Charlton on 26 August 1975. He returned against Scunthorpe in February and scored in that game. He started the next season with both goals against Colchester, ending the season as leading scorer with 20. Here he is sandwiched between a defender and Graham Watson in the 5-1 demolition of Southport on 16 April 1977.

Jim Hall is congratulated by Tom Finney (number ten) after scoring one of his two goals in the 3-0 victory over Doncaster Rovers on 3 May 1977. The win ensured promotion from the Fourth Division with three games left to play. Signed on loan from Northampton at Christmas 1976, Hall scored 15 goals in 24 games.

After United's first ever Football League divisional championship, a special edition of the innovative matchday magazine and programme was produced when the trophy was to be presented. The occasion failed to inspire Cambridge, however, who lost 3-2 to ten-man Swansea.

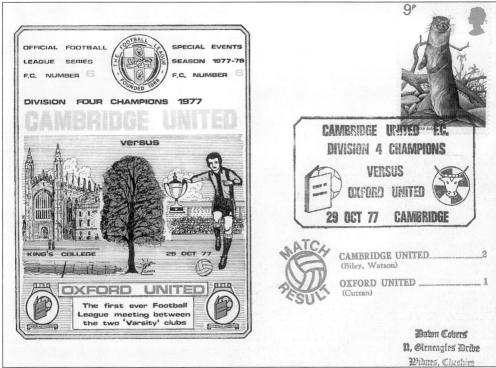

A stamp cover was produced by a national firm to commemorate the first League divisional championship. The game used to illustrate the cover was the 2-1 victory over Oxford in 1977, the first ever meeting in the Football League between the two clubs.

As a direct result of the crowd trouble during the 1977 game against Oxford, the hated ten-foot high fence was erected behind the Newmarket End goal with the away fans penned in at the other end.

The away end fence was put to the test on 2 January 1978, when 10,998 fans saw Cambridge beat Peterborough 1-0. It was a record-breaking ninth consecutive home win and a week later it was announced that Ron Atkinson was leaving to become manager at West Bromwich Albion in the old First Division.

With Ron Atkinson replaced by his number two, John Docherty, Cambridge continued to power towards the Second Division. In April 1978 a bearded Reg Smart met Councillors Powley, Reed, Phillips and a planning official to discuss plans to update the stadium. It was, however, to take another twenty-two years to obtain planning permission to expand onto adjacent Council land.

Later that month, number ten Tom Finney headed in a 73rd minute equaliser against Exeter. With six minutes left in the season, Steve Fallon thumped in another header to take Cambridge United into the Second Division for the first time.

Police first tried out experimental closed circuit TV for crowd monitoring in October 1978 for the first-ever game against Blackburn Rovers. The control point was in the back of a van in the car park.

The squad and apprentices for the 1979/80 Second Division campaign shows Alan Biley (fourth from the left in the third row from the back). He was sold later that season to Derby County for a club record of £450,000. Despite this, United finished eighth – one place above the mighty Newcastle.

In the mud of Chesham in 1979, Roger Gibbins (behind the number two), opened the scoring from Chris Turner's free kick. A second goal from George Reilly set up a game against Aston Villa, and the first appearance of Cambridge United in the fourth round of the FA Cup.

A 1-1 draw with Aston Villa at the Abbey in the FA Cup in January 1980 led to a replay at Villa Park. 36,835 fans, the largest crowd to watch Cambridge United to that date, saw Villa win 4-1. Here, Steve Spriggs celebrates his spectacular 14th minute equaliser.

The main stand extension was built in the summer of 1980, with suites and rooms underneath and 1,600 more seats. With Alan Biley recently sold for nearly twice the cost of the project, the fans immediately nicknamed the £210,000 project 'The Biley Stand'.

Once the roof was on, contractors worked against the clock to get it ready for the first game of the new season. Ironically, it was against Alan Biley's new club, Derby County, who had lost their struggle to stay in the top flight. Every seat was sold as 9,558 saw Cambridge win 3-0 with a goal from Derrick Christie and two from George Reilly – one of which came when he stole the ball from Roy McFarland, the future Cambridge manager.

The wooden hut that was the Black and Amber shop was moved to behind the Newmarket Road end to allow for the extension of the main stand in 1980. The volunteer fans that staffed the shop are seen here displaying the latest wares after the move. From left to right: Alan Burge, Peter Spring, Val Potter, Andy Gilmour, Ivan Potter.

Chelsea's lowest ever League attendance at Stamford Bridge of 6,196 was for the visit of Cambridge in April 1982. Chelsea were easy 4-1 winners, but only ended the season in twelfth place, just two places above Cambridge. With vast empty terraces and stands clearly visible in the background, George Reilly leaps for a cross.

In the absence of the injured Steve Spriggs, the usual penalty taker, Lindsay Smith sent the Chelsea 'keeper Francis the wrong way after Tommy O'Neill was brought down. Smith got the job after scoring 16 out of 16 in training and it was his last goal for Cambridge United before his transfer to Plymouth.

One of the inspirational switches made by John Docherty was to move left winger Jamie Murray to become an attacking full-back. Murray, seen tackling back against Orient in April 1982, made 269 League appearances in two spells at Cambridge.

The 2-0 victory practically ensured survival for Cambridge and relegation for Orient. Watched by Lindsay Smith, Dave Donaldson turns his back as Martin Goldsmith, scorer of both goals, runs back to help.

During the 1982/83 season, no away team scored at the Abbey for five months. On 30 April 1983, John Docherty congratulates Malcolm Webster as he leaves with lynchpin centre-back Chris Turner after the 1-0 defeat of Newcastle. His Football League all-time record of 12 consecutive home clean sheets led to striker George Reilly's comment in the Vice Presidents Club 'Twelve games without a goal? That's nothing. I've gone a lot more than that!'

Six

Plumbing the Depths and Finding a Saviour

1983-90

From the sacking in December 1983 of John Docherty to December 1985, Cambridge United plummeted from the Second Division to the re-election area of Division Four. Chairman David Rushton then found the saviour and made the inspirational appointment of Chris Turner to his first managerial post. The charismatic centre-back had been a firm favourite with the crowd and set about rebuilding the confidence of the team and the fans. Six months after his appointment he sits on the right end of the row of directors in August 1986. He had already made a significant signing – fourth from the left of the second row down is the permed head of his new midfield general, a certain John Beck.

Jamie Murray, Tom Finney, Steve Fallon, Robbie Cooke and Tommy O'Neill made the mascot, Owen Nurse, feel at home in the dressing rooms in 1983.

Between 1978 and 1984, Newcastle came to the Abbey Stadium six times and failed to win on any occasion. Here, Andy Sinton, Cambridge United's youngest ever League player at the age of sixteen, tackles Kevin Keegan.

The end of an era came with the dismissal of John Docherty in December 1983 after a dismal run of results. His replacement, the likeable but inexperienced John Ryan, joined chairman David Rushton for his first match in charge at Charlton where he saw his new charges thrashed 5-2. 'There's 101 things wrong with the team' he announced.

One of the outstanding players inherited by John Ryan was the precocious teenage star Andy Sinton. Here, he beats Mike Flanagan of Charlton watched by Tom Finney – United's first current international, who played for Northern Ireland. Flanagan was later signed for United by Chris Turner and Andy Sinton, who later joined Spurs, became the first ex-United player to play for England.

Commercial manager Dudley Arliss retired in 1984. Widely recognised as the man who built up one of the most successful lottery organisations in football, which had financed the rise of the club, he must have wondered what he was leaving behind. Cambridge United had scored only 3 goals in the 2 draws and 6 losses in their first 8 games under new manager John Ryan.

Paul Daw took over as secretary from Les Holloway in April 1984. His first game was a nightmare. He was punched by Leeds supporters as he tried to sort out problems when they turned up with forged tickets and, in a highly volatile atmosphere, found the police presence weakened because of the miners' strike. Daw later wrote two definitive volumes of the history of the club *United in Endeavour* and *On the Up*.

Cambridge went to the bottom of the Third Division on 22 September 1984 and never moved off it for the rest of the season. Despite this, the club found its first-ever shirt sponsors in February 1985. Steve Fallon and eighteen-year-old Keith Branagan model the new shirts with Miss Cambridge United. A fortnight later, John Ryan was put out of his misery and sacked.

In the early 1980s, the strike force often consisted of Robbie Cooke (*left*) and Martin Goldsmith (*right*). Despite being a prolific goal scorer with other clubs, Cooke could only managed 14 goals in 65 appearances for Cambridge and was sold by Ken Shellito. Goldsmith scored 5 goals in 35 games before being discarded by John Ryan.

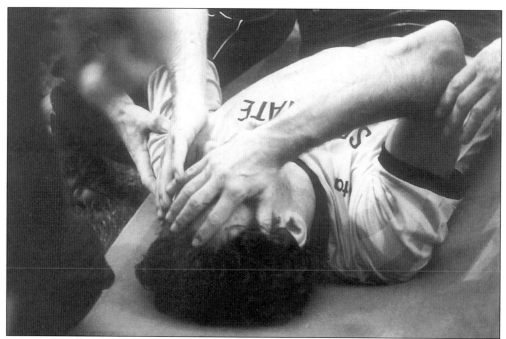

Steve Spriggs (416) and Steve Fallon (410) hold the club record for League appearances. At their joint testimonial against Manchester United in August 1985, Irish international Martin O'Neill played for Cambridge with the view of becoming player-coach. However, he suffered a broken leg which ended his playing days and he later began his managerial career at Wycombe instead.

Mark Hughes, the future manager of Wales, scored at the Newmarket Road end in Manchester United's entertaining 3-2 victory. The other players are, from left to right: guest player Brendon Batson (who later became a highly respected official of the Professional Footballers Association), Frank Stapleton, David Moyes (later to become manager of Preston), goalkeeper Roger Hansbury, Geoff Scott and Mickey Bennett. Alan Biley also guested for Cambridge.

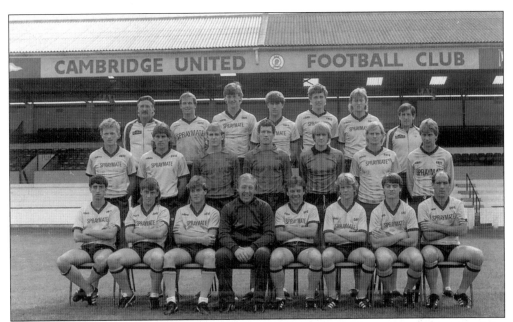

A grinning Ken Shellito and Steve Spriggs appear the only confident ones at the start of the 1985/86 campaign. After two successive relegations, Cambridge United ended the season ignominiously having to apply for re-election to the Football League in a season when they were also dumped out of the FA Cup in the first round by non-League Dagenham.

After defeat by Dagenham, Ken Shellito resigned, saying that he was disillusioned with football. With the club in seemingly terminal decline, Chris Turner was the shock appointment, but in him the club had found the manager to save them. He is seen here making a point to Steve Spriggs at his first training session in December 1985.

Three of the most influential players were sold during the 1987/88 season. Goalkeeper Keith Branagan (back row, third from the right) went to Millwall, with captain Peter Butler and record goalscorer David Crown (fifth and sixth from the left in the front row) going to Southend. United ended the season in fifteenth place.

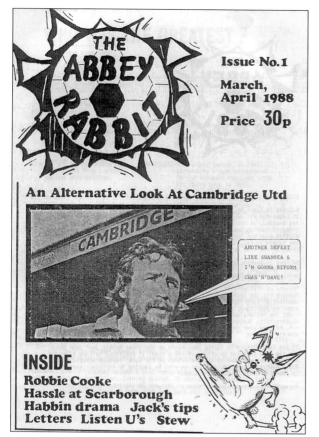

In March 1988 two fans, Nigel Pearce and David Filce, produced the first successful Cambridge fanzine, the popular *Abbey Rabbit* – fifty issues were produced by various editors over the next nine years.

Two mascots are seen with their heroes in 1987 – David Crown, holder of the club record of 27 goals in a Football League season, and Keith Branagan, later to become a Premier League 'keeper with Bolton. Both players made over 100 appearances for Cambridge.

Striker Neil Horwood was the first to congratulate David Crown when he scored his 45th and final goal for Cambridge United in the 4-0 victory over Newport County on 10 October 1987. Later that month, Crown was sold to Southend and at the end of the season Newport lost their League status.

Two players signed in 1988 by Chris Turner were to epitomise the side he built. In the 1989/90 campaign, John Vaughan was the only ever-present, playing 65 games in the season when Cambridge United were promoted by winning the Division Three play-offs. His fearless displays and popularity with the fans won him the accolade of 'The Legend'.

John Taylor made his debut against Leicester in a pre-season friendly on 22 August 1988, having been signed from Sudbury Town. On one memorable occasion in March 1989 he scored in a victory over Colchester, then was cheered to the echo for a faultless last sixteen minutes in goal, after John Vaughan had been badly injured in a freak accident with his own centre-back Phil Chapple.

Seven
Beck's Rollercoaster
1990-93

Dion Dublin and John Taylor scored 40 of the 91 goals in the 1990/91 Third Division championship season. Cambridge United also reached the quarter-finals of the FA Cup for the second year running during that campaign.

Chris Turner handed the reins, and the exciting squad of players he had built, to his assistant John Beck in January 1990. Gary Johnson, ex-manager of Newmarket Town, stepped up from managing the reserves to become Beck's number two. When John Beck returned as manager for the second time in 2001, Gary Johnson was by then the national coach of Latvia.

As Cambridge prepared for the quarter-finals of the FA Cup in 1990, Gary Johnson said 'They say every season someone's name is on the FA Cup. It can't be ours … can it?' John Taylor modelled the 'CUFC Wembley Tour 1990' T-shirt, but Crystal Palace ended the dream with a scruffy 79th minute goal.

Cambridge clinched a Fourth Division play-off place with a 2-0 victory at Aldershot on 5 May 1990. Winger Lee Philpott, seen here applauding the 2,000 travelling fans after the final whistle, was substituted to bring on defender Danny O'Shea after centre-back Liam Daish was sent off.

Maidstone were the opponents over two legs in the play-offs. After a draw at the Abbey, Cambridge won on an emotional night at Maidstone with two goals in extra time. Here, Phil Chapple challenges at a Cambridge corner in the first leg, watched by Liam Daish.

John Beck and his captain, Phil Chapple, lead the team out for the Third Division play-off final on 26 May 1990. Cambridge played Chesterfield at Wembley Stadium in front of 26,440 fans.

In the 77th minute, Colin Bailie won a corner chasing a lost cause. Dion Dublin beat the 'keeper and two defenders to head in Chris Leadbitter's cross for the only goal of the game.

After two nervous minutes of injury time, during which Danny O'Shea blocked a goal-bound shot from a Chesterfield corner, referee George Courtney blew his whistle to end the game. Dion Dublin looks to the heavens as the Cambridge bench run onto the pitch.

The scoreboard summed it all up as the fans waited for the lap of honour.

Dion Dublin parades the play-off trophy wearing a Cambridge United cap he acquired on the walk up the famous thirty-nine steps to the presentation box. He later swapped the cap for a black and amber stove-pipe top hat with moose antlers.

86

After winning the play-off final at Wembley, an open-topped coach took the squad to a civic reception at the Guildhall. Just as they had twenty years previously when the City last honoured the team, fans packed the Market Square to greet them.

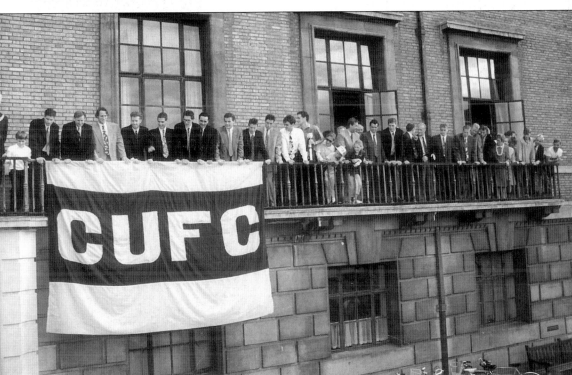

When everyone came out to take the applause, the flag specially made to fly over Wembley hung from the Guildhall balcony.

In August 1989, a fan rushed straight from the airport to a game and told his friends 'Stay away from me. I must smell like a moose'. He was welcomed with chants of 'Moose!' and antler finger-waving. Astonishingly, the bit of fun swept through the terraces and soon even the players were joining in: The Moose was born. At the 1990 civic reception, the players 'Moosed' the fans from the Guildhall balcony. From left to right: Mick Cook, Andy Fensome, John Taylor, Chris Leadbitter, John Vaughan, Steve Claridge.

Someone even donated a moose head for a 1990 fundraising auction. John Taylor, Chris Leadbitter and Dion Dublin joined the fans showing their purchases. The Vice Presidents Club paid £500 for the Wembley match ball, only for it to disappear from their clubroom.

Abbey Action, a group founded by fundraising fans in 1980, presented the club with a new flag to fly over the Abbey in 1990. From left to right: David Smith (Abbey Action chairman), Colin Smith, Simon Cousins, Clive Dawson, Reg Smart (Cambridge United chairman).

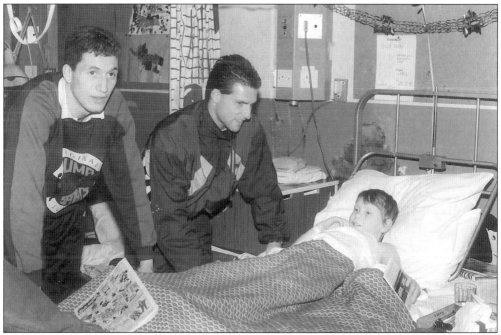

Phil Chapple and Andy Fensome were among the players on Christmas Eve 1990 making the traditional Christmas visit to the children's ward at Addenbrookes Hospital. The little boy is proudly clutching the Cambridge United 1991 diary they have just given him that contained photographs of the players.

The Cambridge fans queued for hours to get into Highbury for the quarter-final of the FA Cup against Arsenal on 8 March 1991, when 10,000 of them made the trip.

Dion Dublin beats Tony Adams, the ball looping over David Seaman to make it 1-1. Unfortunately, Tony Adams got the Arsenal winner in the second half in front of 42,973 fans – the largest crowd Cambridge had ever played in front of.

When the whistle blew after a 2-0 victory over Swansea at Cambridge on 11 May 1991, United were champions of the Third Division. Danny O'Shea and Graham Scarff leap out of the dug-out to begin the celebrations. The trophy had been taken to Southend to present to them, but a huge roar from the 9,000 crowd in the second half shook the Abbey as the fans heard on their radios that Brentford had scored at Southend. The two results gave Cambridge the title by one point.

The Optimist of the Year award went to the Tannoy announcer, who asked towards the end of the 1991 championship-winning game 'If the score stays the same at Southend, please do not invade the pitch at the end.' Celebrations that night included one at John Beck's house for the players and in the Vice Presidents Club, where many thousands of pounds had been won by members who had accepted Ladbrookes pre-season odds of 33-1 against Cambridge winning the title.

John Beck leads by example on Coldhams Common in the heat of July as the players prepared for the 1991/92 campaign on their return to the old Second Division. They powered their way to five straight wins when the season opened.

With his meticulous approach to every aspect of the game, and an emphasis on super fitness, nobody dared come back to the taskmaster unfit or overweight. Richard Wilkins, Colin Sinclair, Lee Philpott and Dion Dublin lead the front line.

John Beck's 100th game in charge was a bruising encounter at Millwall in September 1991. Steve Claridge runs at the defence with Michael Cheetham, Andy Fensome and Colin Bailie in support.

The goal that everyone remembers won that game as United came back from 1-0 down. Millwall fans and players looked on in disbelief when Lee Philpott's cross was met by seventeen-year-old substitute Gary Rowett on his debut, hanging in the air then powering in a header with such force that it jammed between the stanchion and the net.

The dream draw in the Rumbelows Cup in September 1991 came with a two-legged tie against Manchester United. At Old Trafford, John Taylor takes on Mike Phelan with Neil Webb running back. Manchester United made the second leg academic with a brilliant 3-0 victory described by Alex Ferguson as 'some of our very best football.'

A terrace hero in a long line of totally committed Cambridge United midfielders, Colin Bailie is seen here at Portsmouth in 1991. Typically, he has had the shirt nearly pulled off his back in an attempt to stop him. He retired from the game in 1992 to join the police force.

Swindon's player-manager, Glen Hoddle (in the number four shirt), looks on in disbelief after Nicky Summerbee has put the ball in his own net. Lee Philpott's corner had caused chaos at the Newmarket Road end during a comprehensive Cambridge victory in 1991.

On the way to Charlton in 1991, Tony Dennis and Dion Dublin tried to work out how to play the Cambridge United board game. Dublin scored in the 2-0 victory that kept Cambridge on top of the old Second Division. The following summer, Dublin became the first £1 million Cambridge player with his transfer to Manchester United.

For sixteen years as chairman, from 1974 to 1990, David Rushton's financial skills and dry sense of humour kept the club afloat in good times and bad. He was also the man behind the intuitive appointment of Chris Turner as manager after the club had sunk to twenty-first in the Fourth Division in December 1985. Appointed president in 1990, he is seen here in the dressing rooms in the 1992/93 season, when his health had began to deteriorate. He died in August 1993.

As John Beck tightened the absolute rigidity of his game plan, the notorious 'QUALITY' boards were erected to show the players the areas they had to aim for with every forward ball. With the Newmarket Road end marker in the background, Port Vale's goalkeeper, Mark Grew, collects a typical cross in April 1992.

Phil Chapple and Danny O'Shea at Sunderland in May 1992. The 2-2 draw saw United end the season in fifth place and paired with Leicester in the play-offs for a place in the Premier League. After a draw at the Abbey in the first leg, the dream was shattered with a 5-0 wipe-out at Filbert Street.

With growing accusations of gamesmanship and dubious tactics, Cambridge had difficulties in finding opponents for the traditional pre-season match for the Cambs Professional Cup in 1992. Chester finally agreed to take part and inflicted an embarrassing defeat. Here, Danny O'Shea gets his shirt pulled by a defender on the blind side of the referee.

After a summer of player discontent, walk-outs, transfers, and contract wrangles, the 1992/93 squad showed significant changes. United lost their first four League games. The exciting rollercoaster had finally come off the rails and it was the beginning of the end for John Beck.

Eight

Managerial
Merry-Go-Round
1993-97

Gary Johnson's first competitive match after his appointment as manager in 1993 was against a full strength Nottingham Forest in the Cambs Professional Cup. The Forest fans saw 'keeper Jon Sheffield at his best, returning after a broken leg. Stan Collymore scored twice on his Forest debut, but Steve Butler also got two and Liam Daish headed in the Cambridge winner.

After John Beck was sacked in October 1992, caretaker-manager Gary Johnson fired up both the team and the fans, even buying back terrace hero Steve Claridge. Controversially, the Board appointed Ian Atkins as Beck's replacement. Even Claridge could not save Atkins, however, despite this win at Brentford (where he got booked for having his socks rolled down as usual).

By May 1993 at West Ham, time was running out for Ian Atkins. Desperation set in and hypnotist George Lord was recruited. United lost and were relegated, and Ian Atkins was sacked after twenty-three weeks, the shortest ever tenure of any manager at the club for forty years.

After sacking Ian Atkins the Board installed Gary Johnson as manager, with chairman Reg Smart admitting to a fans forum that it had been a mistake not to have given him the job instead of Ian Atkins. The loss of revenue due to the relegation forced the club to sell Alan Kimble to Wimbledon, Paul Raynor to Preston, Chris Leadbitter to Bournemouth and Phil Chapple to Charlton.

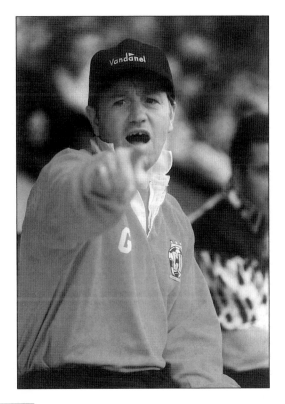

Gary Johnson's first major signing was Dean Barrick from Rotherham, as he looked to move to a wing-back system. In the opening League game, Cambridge played Blackpool for the first time ever and in the words of Blackpool manager Dave Bamber 'They slaughtered us'. Here, Barrick is shown cooling himself down on that sweltering hot day.

A Burnley attacker finds himself the meat in a Cambridge United centre-back sandwich in October 1993. Mick Heathcote is on the bottom and Liam Daish, later to be sold to Coventry, on the top. Liam Daish became an Irish international before injury prematurely ended his League career.

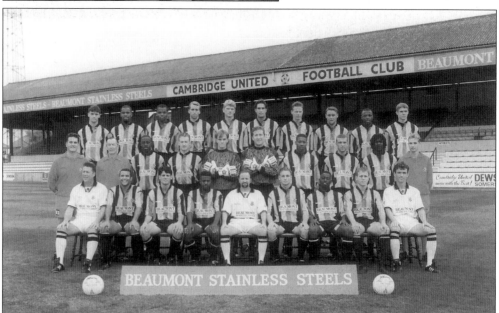

The squad for the 1994/95 season shows the youth team manager, Tommy Taylor, on the left of the front row. He was to take over when Johnson was fired in April after one win in fourteen games had left United looking down the barrel of relegation. Three wins and a draw in the last six games fail to save them, despite ending fifth from bottom – that season five clubs were sent down in divisional rearrangements.

In 1994, Charlie and Glad Owen, along with their daughter and grandson, won the national Dedicated Family Sporting Award to commemorate a lifetime of service to the club. The legendary activities of the Owen family ranged from painting the terraces in their holidays, to the FA Cup match against Aston Villa in 1980, when Glad won a bottle of champagne from the chairman, having accepted his wager that she could not sell £1,000 worth of raffle tickets in one afternoon.

Lil Harrison was a dedicated supporter of the club for over seventy years. In the early 1920s she helped carry the goal posts to Stourbridge Common before every game. She recalled cattle grazing in the field that the present Abbey Stadium was built on when the team played at a nearby piece of land called the Celery Trenches. Present at every major event in the history of Abbey and Cambridge United, Lil served on the management committee of the Supporters Club for over thirty years and every Christmas organised one of the biggest raffles in East Anglia. She is seen here at the Player of the Year event in 1994 in her ninetieth year.

Watched by Prime Minister John Major, Jason Lillis put Cambridge 2-1 ahead against Peterborough at London Road on New Year's Eve 1994. He joined the United fans in celebration, but late in the game Ken Charlery got the Peterborough equaliser.

'Worse than a nightmare' is how manager Gary Johnson described the record 6-0 defeat at Brentford in 1995. Here, Steve Butler collects a punch in the head from ex-United 'keeper Kevin Dearden. Dave Campbell, playing his first game for Cambridge, suffered a broken leg which ended his career, and Billy Manuel got sent off for the third time in five games.

With relegation looming, Cambridge were under new management in April 1995. Tommy Taylor and his number two Paul Clark took over from Gary Johnson. In the background is kit man Roger Parker.

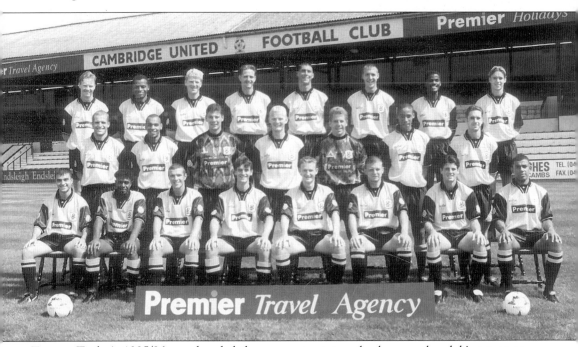

Tommy Taylor's 1995/96 squad ended the season in sixteenth place on the club's return to Division Three. Taylor made a significant signing in March of that season, getting Paul Wanless on a free transfer from the Lincoln manager, John Beck.

Tommy Taylor presented Steve Butler with his Player of the Year award in 1995. The previous season, Butler's golden glut of goals included a club record five at Exeter, three hat-tricks in a month and eight goals in two consecutive games.

Steve Butler adds the second in the 2-0 defeat of Peterborough in Tommy Taylor's first game in charge, in April 1995.

Cambridge celebrated twenty-five years in the Football League in 1995. Canadian international Carlo Corazzin is modelling the souvenir shirt. He was sold in March 1996 to Plymouth for £150,000.

Matt Joseph, in 1996, is seen here chasing down Barnet left-back Jamie Campbell, who himself had two spells with Cambridge United. Campbell returned in 1997 to play left-back in Roy McFarland's team after Matt Joseph had moved to Orient to rejoin Tommy Taylor.

Avid fans, journalist Janet Williams and Mark Johnson, produced the *Football Fans' Guide*, a definitive guide for travelling fans to every Football League ground in the country in 1995. In 2001 the match programme produced by Mark Johnson, by now the club's assistant secretary, was given the award of Best Programme in Division Two and came eighth in the national ratings of the 92 League clubs.

Carlo Corazzin feels the weight of the Hereford 'keeper in 1995. In both this season and the previous one he was the leading goalscorer. Corazzin, signed by Gary Johnson, scored 41 goals in his 113 appearances for Cambridge.

The 1996/97 squad included Micah Hyde (left end of the middle row), Danny Granville (third from the right of the middle row) and Jody Craddock (right hand end of the back row), who were all shortly to play in the Premiership with Watford, Chelsea and Sunderland respectively.

The man they loved to hate was Scott McGleish. Here he runs into the net after his 87th-minute equaliser against Rochdale in 1996, when seventeen-year-old goalkeeper Shaun Marshall made his debut. McGleish cracked in 7 goals in 11 appearances when on loan from Peterborough, then refused to sign when Tommy Taylor left to take over at Orient.

In 1996 the cult TV Sports quiz *They Think It's All Over* started showing bizarre goal celebrations and asked what was going on. In order to get on the show, the team invented the Elephant Walk, first seen to celebrate a Paul Raynor goal. The ploy worked and they later recreated it for the cameras.

Tony Richards found some intellectual reading to pass the time during the long trip to Torquay in 1996. It inspired him to give one of his best displays in a Cambridge shirt before being substituted by sixteen-year-old Trevor Benjamin in the 3-0 victory.

Nine

The Time of
The Big Mac

1997-2001

Assistant manager David Preece celebrates promotion at Rochdale on 27 April 1999 with
Aston Villa loanee Richard Walker and captain Paul Wanless.

After the acrimonious departure of Tommy Taylor to Orient amidst a welter of accusations and counter-accusations between him and the Board over his contract, the ex-Derby County and England centre-back Roy McFarland was appointed in November 1996.

As Roy McFarland faced the task of winning over the fans, he asked them to 'Judge me by my signings'. One of his first was Martin Butler from Walsall for a bargain £22,000. Here, Butler soars above the Macclesfield defender Sodje in 1997 in the first meeting of the two clubs. Macclesfield won 3-1 on their way to promotion.

'If you cut him, he bleeds black and amber' was how the fans described Paul Wanless. In typically determined mood, he is shown here charging the Fulham defence in May 1997. On the left are Trevor Benjamin, Marc Joseph and Micah Hyde, with referee Terry Heilbron in close attendance.

Roy McFarland's squad for the 1997/98 season went top of Division Three in September, then failed to win any of the following thirteen games. The inspirational Paul Wanless was made captain during the season in which four different supporters' groups voted him their Player of the Year.

Commercial manager Carla Frediani and Renford Sargeant announced the renewal of the club sponsorship by Premier Travel in 1997. Renford Sargeant later became a director of Cambridge United.

In 1997 the club undertook an ambitious scheme to ensure all their matchday stewards were fully trained and qualified. Stadium manager Ian Darler is seen here with some of his sixty-nine stewards who were awarded National Vocational Qualifications sports safety certificates.

Club secretary Steve Greenall left United in 1998 to take over as press officer at Norwich City. He handed over to his successor, ex-United apprentice Andy Pincher, who had stayed on as assistant secretary after being forced out of League football by injury problems.

The team trying jelly-babies, reported to being good for energy levels, before the game against Brentford in December 1998. From left to right: Ben Chenery, Ian Ashbee, Andy Duncan, Roy McFarland, Jamie Campbell, Martin Butler, Alex Russell, Trevor Benjamin. They lost the game 1-0 to an outrageous fifty-yard lob after five minutes of play.

Commentators Kenneth Woolstenholme and John Motson presented commercial manager Carla Frediani and director Roger Hunt with the Colman's 1998 Football Food Award for the best food in the Football League. That season the *Total Football* magazine voted the Abbey the best ground for away supporters – taking into account facilities, quality of food, friendliness and atmosphere.

Public relations manager Graham Eales feeds the legendary bacon rolls to celebrity football supporters Rory McGrath and Elvis, with varying degrees of success.

Sportsmen dinners were started by the Abbey Action fundraisers in the 1980s, with famous guest speakers, and soon became popular events. Roy McFarland and Alan Mullery got the treatment from Bob 'The Cat' Bevan at a Sportsmen Dinner held in the Harris Suite in 1998.

e club built an enviable reputation for encouraging children over the years. The Junior U's he 1970s and '80s became Marvin's Moose Crew in the '90s, with their own page in the ramme. Here, happiness is Moose loose in the family enclosure in 1998.

Past stars were invited back to the Abbey in April 2000. From left to right: Richard Wilkins, Laurie Ryan, Andy Beattie, Trevor Howard, Graham Watson, George Reilly, Terry Eades, Malcolm Lindsey, Brian Moore, Peter Phillips, Rodney Slack.

Steve Fallon, Malcolm Webster, Steve Spriggs, and Alan Biley were all signed by Ron Atkinson for a nominal outlay. Between them they made 1,250 League appearances for Cambridge United. The boy in the photograph is Stephen Spriggs Junior, who already plays for Cambridge United youth sides.

In the 1990s the Internet revolution led to the opening of an unofficial web site by exiled fan Andrea Thrussell, living in the Isle of Man. An Internet network of fans was also set up called Moosenet. Each season they travelled from all over the British Isles and even abroad to meet up at a game. Director Gary Harwood and Michael Kyd (on the right) join Andrea and the Moosenetters at their 1999 get-together.

With promotion assured at Rochdale in 1999 with three games left, Neil Mustoe, Trevor Benjamin and Ben Chenery could not believe their ears when John Taylor entertained them on the coach coming home. Taylor scored both goals in the 2-0 victory.

Katherine and Paul Wanless present one of the many cheques for money raised by them and the fans for the Hinchingbrooke Hospital Special Care Baby Unit, where baby Emily spent the first few months of her life. Brenda Hanna accepts the cheque before the Bury game in April 1999. The proud father opened the scoring in the 3-0 victory.

World Cup final referee Jack Taylor presented Ian Darler with his 1998/99 award for becoming Division Three Groundsman of the Year. Over three decades the condition of his pitches has won constant praise. In 1988 the manager of Leicester, David Pleat, told reporters 'Have you seen the state of that pitch? They should do something about it – like give it to me.'

Cambridge Evening News reporter Randall Butt first started reporting on Cambridge United fixtures in 1974. Here he chats to Roy McFarland, the eleventh manager whose teams he had covered at Cambridge, not counting the caretakers.

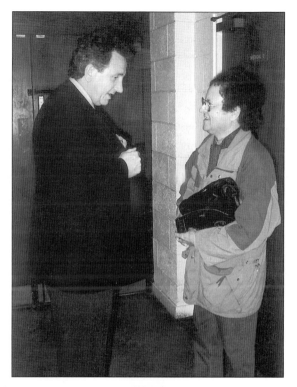

Roy McFarland and chairman Reg Smart were in contemplative mood, having just seen Brentford snatch the Division Three championship from them. The two sides met at the Abbey in the final match of the season in May 1999 in a title showdown.

At the start of the 1999/2000 season, Trevor Benjamin seemed to be confused at the photo shoot. At the end of the season he was leading scorer with 23 goals and transferred that summer to Leicester for £1.5 million – a record fee for a Cambridge player.

As the season drew to an end, for the first time six ex-Youth team players were named in the first-team line up. From left to right, wearing the away strip, are: Shaun Marshall, Marc Joseph, Trevor Benjamin, Tom Youngs, Martin McNeil, Adam Tann.

Crystal Palace were swept aside in the third round of the FA Cup on 10 December 1999 in one of the best displays of the season. Paul Wanless disappears under his team-mates as he makes it 2-0 after 83 minutes.

The squad were in a happy mood in February 2000 before the trip to Notts County. Twice they came from behind to win 3-2 for the season's first away league victory. Trevor Benjamin's injury-time winner began a late surge that staved off relegation.

John Taylor salutes the fans in May 2000 at the end of the season in which he scored his 100th goal for the club. The previous season he had beaten Alan Biley's League goals record and been voted into the Football League's Hall of Fame as the fans' favourite player of all time.

When John Taylor burst onto the scene in 1988, the gangling youngster with the mop of unruly hair was christened 'Shaggy' by the fans, who thought he looked like the character of that name in the children's TV cartoon *Scooby -Doo*. Twelve years later, the graffiti on a wall outside the Abbey Stadium summed up their feelings towards him.

Ten

Moving into the Twenty-first Century

Reg Smart and the fans celebrated outside Cambridge Guildhall in March 2000 when the Council finally approved plans for the redevelopment of the Abbey Stadium after the club's twenty-five years of campaigning to obtain modern facilities.

Chairman Reg Smart was at the Newmarket Road end to greet Lionel Perez in August 2000. The flamboyant French 'keeper was given a hero's welcome by the fans after his loan spell had resulted in a permanent signing from Newcastle.

Cambridge Fans United – the supporters organisation founded to help fund the redevelopment and support the club's involvement in community activities – was launched on 31 August 2000. From left to right: Anne Campbell MP, Trevor Peer (Radio Cambridgeshire), Nick Pomery (CFU chairman), Gary Atyes (CFU committee member).

With plans for the new stadium approved and the final legal obstacles removed, the club launched schemes to raise the money. Directors and employees of Spicers handed over £21,500 to chairman Reg Smart in November 2000 to purchase the first executive box in the rebuilt stadium.

With just 3 wins in the last 23 League games, the Board sacked Roy McFarland and on 1 March 2001 announced the controversial return of John Beck. The subsequent 5 wins and 3 draws in the remaining 13 games saved the club from seemingly certain relegation. In May, John Beck presented the Player of the Year award to Paul Wanless, who for the second time won four top awards in a single season.

The day after the 2000/2001 season ended, work began on the phased £4.4 million project to redevelop the ground into a modern 10,000 capacity all-seater stadium, as shown on the architect's plans *(below)*.

CAMBRIDGE UNITED F.C.

PROPOSED GROUND REDEVELOPMENT
ABBEY STADIUM, NEWMARKET ROAD
CAMBRIDGE
CAMBRIDGE UNITED FOOTBALL CLUB